You Can Minister In God's Power

A Guide for Spirit-filled Disciples

Denzil R. Miller

This books is a condensation and adaptation of the author's book, *Power Encounter: Ministering in the Power and Anointing of the Holy Spirit.*

All scripture quotations, unless otherwise noted, are taken from the HOLY BIBLE, NEW INTERNATIONAL VERSION, copyright 1973, 1978, 1984 by the International Bible Society. All rights reserved.

Libraries of Congress Cataloging-in-Publication Data
Miller, Denzil R., 1946–
You Can Minister in God's Power
Denzil R. Miller

ISBN: 978-0-9911332-5-3

1. Teaching—Pentecostal 2. Biblical teaching— 3. Biblical studies—
Holy Spirit— Healing— Miracles

Printed in the United States of America
PneumaLife Publications
Springfield, MO 65803

– Contents –

Introduction 5

Lesson 1:   Power Ministry Defined 7

Lesson 2:   Power Ministry Illustrated 11

Lesson 3:   Power Ministry and the Kingdom of God 15

Lesson 4:   Power Ministry and Preaching the Gospel 19

Lesson 5:   Preparation for a Power Ministry 23

Lesson 6:   The Baptism in the Holy Spirit and

Power Ministry 27

Lesson 7:   Gifts of the Holy Spirit and Power Encounter . . . 31

Lesson 8:   Divine Guidance and Power Encounter 35

Lesson 9:   The Weapons of Our Warfare, Part 1 39

Lesson 10: The Weapons of Our Warfare, Part 2 43

Lesson 11: How to Heal the Sick 47

Lesson 12: How to Cast out Demons 51

Lesson 13: How to Pray with Believers to be Filled

with the Spirit 55

Appendix 59

Other Books By the Author 60

– Introduction –

A missionary colleague of mine once told me of an experience of his. He had met a man on the streets of Mexico City. When he introduced himself as an Assemblies of God missionary, the man became very excited and said, "Oh yes! You belong to that church that is growing so fast!"

"We thank God for His blessings," the missionary replied.

"I know why you are growing so fast," the man continued.

"How is that?" my friend asked.

"It's because you make all of your members into preachers!"

Well, that statement is partly true. If by "preachers" the man meant ordained professional ministers, he was wrong. But if he means that the church had effectively empowered, equipped, and released its laity to be active participants in the work of God, we truly hope that what he said was true.

It is my conviction that such a model should be the norm for ministry in the church. God expects all of His children to be active preachers of the gospel, that is, active participants in reaching and discipling others to follow Christ. Among Jesus' last words to His church before ascending into heaven were,

> This is what is written: The Christ will suffer and rise from the dead on the third day, and repentance and forgiveness of sins will be preached in his name to all nations, beginning at Jerusalem. *You are witnesses of these things.* (Acts 24:46-48, emphasis added)

We have all been called to be witnesses to the death and resurrection of Christ. This is Christ's mandate for all Christians (Matt. 28:18-20; Mark 16:15-16; John 20:21-22).

We should be encouraged, however, because Christ has not left us to accomplish the work on our own. He has promised us all the power we need to fulfill the task, for, in the very next verse, Jesus promised, "I am going to send you what my Father has promised; but stay in the city until you have been clothed with power from on high" (v. 49; see also Acts 1:4-8). This promised power enables Christ's disciples to share the gospel with great effectiveness. It also enables them to minister with powerful signs following. Every believer, if he or she will appropriate Christ's promise, and learn the principles of power ministry, can minister in God's power. This includes you! *You, too, can minister in God's power!*

The lessons in this book are designed to lead you into such a ministry. They are a condensation and adaption of the lessons found in my earlier book, *Power Encounter: How to Minister in the Power and Anointing of the Holy Spirit.* If you want greater insight into the issues discussed here, I recommend that you get a copy of that book.

The design of these lessons is threefold: First, they seek to lay a biblical foundation for a ministry of power. It is only on such a firm biblical foundation that a credible ministry in the Spirit can be built. This issue is addressed in Lessons 1-4. Next, they deal with the personal preparation one needs in order to minister in the power of the Holy Spirit. These issues are addressed in Lessons 5-6. Finally, the book seeks to offer practical advice on how one may actually *do* power ministry. This is the aim of Lessons 7-13.

It is my sincere desire that these lessons will serve as a practical, on-the-job training manual for those who sincerely seek to obey the command of Jesus to preach the gospel with signs following (Mark 16:15-20).

— Denzil R. Miller

Power Ministry Defined

Central Truth
To be truly effective in ministry we must learn to minister in the power and anointing of the Holy Spirit.

Lesson Outline
• The Need for a Power Ministry
• The Terms Defined

Introduction
When Jesus returned to heaven He did not leave His church powerless. He gave to it all the power it needed to evangelize the entire world (Acts 1:8). He first fulfilled that promise on the Day of Pentecost when He poured out the Holy Spirit on the waiting disciples (Acts 2:1-4). As a result, the New Testament church went out and ministered in great power and with amazing results. Some have described the method of the early church as power evangelism. In this lesson we will introduce this concept.

THE NEED FOR A POWER MINISTRY

As did the early church, the church today needs power if it is to fulfill its God-given mandate of discipling all nations before the soon coming of Christ (Matt. 24:14; 28:18-20). There are at least four reasons the church must have a ministry filled with God's power:

We Are Involved in a War
The Bible clearly teaches that we who call ourselves disciples of Jesus are involved in a great spiritual war. We wage this war against the devil and his legions (Matt. 13:39, see also Luke 10:19). Paul spoke of this spiritual conflict: "For our struggle is not against flesh and blood, but against the rulers, against the authorities, against the powers of this dark world and against the spiritual forces of evil in the heavenly realms" (Eph. 6:12). Paul further wrote that we must use powerful spiritual weapons to successfully wage this spiritual warfare (2 Cor. 10:4).

The Enemy Has Power

Jesus spoke of "all the power of the enemy" (Luke 10:19). Satan has at his disposal a vast and dedicated army of demonic forces who oppose the spread of the gospel (2 Cor. 4:4). If we are to defeat the devil, we must meet his power with even greater power, that is, the power of the Holy Spirit.

The Task Is Great

The task that Jesus has given to us—that is, preaching the gospel in all the world— is so great that it can only be done in the Spirit's power (Matt. 24:14; 28:19-20; Mark 16:15-16). Billions worldwide have not had an adequate witness of the gospel. Many of these people live in lands controlled by religious systems opposed the spread of Christianity. Jesus, nevertheless, promised us power to accomplish this task (Acts 1:8). He said that, as we go to preach the gospel, He would confirm His word with signs following (Mark16:15-17).

Power Ministry Works

A final reason we must be involved in power ministry is because power ministry works. The tremendous success of the early church can be attributed in large part to the fact that it moved in supernatural power. The same is true today. Some have pointed out that globally 70% of all church growth is among Pentecostal and charismatic groups, that is, those who believe in and expect the power of the Holy Spirit to be manifested their ministries.

If we want to see New Testament results in our evangelistic efforts today, we must employ New Testament methods. We must learn to minister in the power and anointing of the Holy Spirit.

THE TERMS DEFINED

To better understand power ministry it is helpful to understand the terms associated with such a ministry. Let's look at five:

Power Ministry

Power ministry is any ministry in the supernatural, originating with the Spirit of God, used to advance the kingdom of God in the earth. It includes signs, wonders, healings, anointed preaching, the casting out of demons, the ministry of spiritual gifts, or any other manifestations of God's power or presence. *Power encounter* often involves confronting demons in the power of Jesus' name and in the power of the Holy Spirit. Throughout this study we will be using the terms power ministry and power encounter interchangeably.

Truth Encounter

A *truth encounter* is any clear declaration of the gospel of Jesus Christ accompanying a power encounter. While a power encounter challenges the powers of darkness, a truth encounter challenges the false teachings of a religion or society holding people in bondage. It is essential that a truth encounter always accompany a power encounter. This topic will be discussed more fully in Lesson 4.

Power Healing

Covenant healing is healing provided through Christ's atoning work on the cross (Isa. 53:4-5; Matt. 8:16-17). This is the healing that He has provided for God's covenant people; that is, those who have made Christ their Lord and Savior. Jesus called this kind of healing "the children's bread" (Matt. 15:25). *Power healing* is healing used to demonstrate the presence of God's kingdom. Here God heals even nonbelievers. Used together with the proclamation of the gospel, this kind of healing confirms that what is preached is true. It is sometimes called "signs and wonders" in the gospels and Acts.

Power Evangelism

Power evangelism results when power encounter is combined with truth encounter. It can be illustrated as follows:

Power Encounter + Truth Encounter = Power Evangelism

Power evangelism takes place when there is a demonstration of God's supernatural power *plus* a clear, convincing presentation of the gospel.

Signs and Wonders

The term *signs and wonders* is often used in the New Testament in relation to evangelism (Acts 4:29-30; 5:12; 6:8; 14:3; Rom.15:19; Heb. 2:3-4). A sign is miraculous happening that points to the fact that the kingdom of God has come, and that the message of the gospel is true (Mark 16:15, 20). As we go to preach the gospel, we can expect God to confirm the message with signs following. A wonder speaks of a miraculous work of God that causes the beholder to marvel—as when Jesus healed the demonized boy (Luke 9:43).

In Acts the wonder of the people included utter amazement (2:7; 3:10), being filled with awe (2:43), perplexity (2:12), hearts filled with praise to God (4:21), great fear (5:5, 11), great joy (8:8), astonishment (8:13), and even saving faith (9:42, see also 1 Cor. 2:4-5). We should sincerely pray that signs and wonders will accompany our preaching today, just as they did the preaching of the early believers (Acts 4:30: 8:6).

Spirit-empowered preaching accompanied by supernatural signs and wonders is a vital key to our reaching the world with the gospel. We must, therefore, understand clearly what it means to minister in the power of the Holy Spirit with signs following. As we do, we will begin to see New Testaments results in our evangelistic and church planting efforts. This is the purpose of this study, that we may know these things. As you read and study the following lessons, I pray that, through faith and openness to the Holy Spirit, you, too, will begin to minister in New Testament power and with New Testaments results.

Class Discussion

Discuss the following in class:

1. Why is it important that we not use "the weapons of the world" to fight spiritual battles? Discuss the weapons that we must use.
2. Explain why the task of the church is so great that we need a power ministry to accomplish it.
3. List and discuss the various terms used to describe power ministry.
4. Many today are trying to reach the world in their own strength and through human methods alone. What do you think their efforts?

– Lesson 2 –
Power Ministry Illustrated

Central Truth
Power encounters can be found throughout the Old and New Testaments, and can serve as examples of how we can minister today.

Lesson Outline
- Power Encounter in the Old Testament
- Power Encounter in the Ministry of Jesus
- Power Encounter in the Ministry of the Early Church

Introduction
In Lesson 1 we defined and defended power ministry. In this lesson we will illustrate it by citing several biblical examples. This will help us to see what power encounters look like in actual practice.

POWER ENCOUNTER IN THE OLD TESTAMENT

The Old Testament contains many exciting examples of power encounter. Let's look at two:

Moses' Challenge to the "gods" of Egypt
Read the story of how Moses challenged the pagan "gods" of Egypt in Exodus 7-13. As you read, remember that God told Moses that these confrontations between him and Pharaoh were actually encounters between God and "all the gods of Egypt" (Exod. 12:12). According to Paul, these gods were, in fact, demons (1 Cor. 10:20). Through the ten plagues, God was systematically attacking the false gods of Egypt. These gods were demonic principalities holding the people in spiritual bondage. The exodus of the children of Israel from Egyptian bondage was more than just a physical deliverance for God's people, it was also a demonstration of their spiritual deliverance from the powers of darkness, and of their freedom to worship Jehovah alone.

Elijah's Challenge to the Prophets of Baal

Read the exciting story of the power encounter between Elijah and the demonically inspired Canaanite god, Baal (1 Kings 18:20-46). On this occasion Elijah was not only confronting the pagan religion of Baal worship, he was also confronting the demons who were behind the religion, giving it its power. This confrontation was both a power encounter and a truth encounter (1 Kings 18:21). Elijah used the miracle as an opportunity to preach to the people and to call upon them to follow the true and living God!

POWER ENCOUNTER IN THE MINISTRY OF JESUS

Jesus' ministry was filled with power encounters. Through these demonstrations of power Jesus showed that He truly was the "Anointed One," the Messiah, sent from God. He also showed that the kingdom of God had come to overthrow the kingdom of Satan (Luke 11:20). Power encounter is seen in the ministry of Jesus in four ways:

In the Purpose of His Ministry

One reason Jesus came was "to destroy the devil's work" (1 John 3:8). Even the demons understood this (Mark 1:23-24). Jesus announced that His ministry would involve six elements: anointing, preaching, setting the prisoners free, healing, releasing the oppressed, and proclaiming the coming of the kingdom of God (Luke 4:18-19).

In the Performance of His Ministry

The twofold emphasis of Jesus' ministry was on proclamation and demonstration (Matt. 4:23; 9:35). He thus combined power encounter with truth encounter in His ministry strategy. Let's look at three typical examples of this ministry strategy of Jesus:

1. His first miracle in Mark (Read Mark 1:21-27; see also 34, 39; 3:10-11). On this occasion Jesus commanded the demons to "Be quiet!" and "Come out!" They had no choice but to obey!

2. His encounter with the Gadarene demoniac (Read Mark 5:1-20). This story is the most complete example in the gospels of Jesus confronting and defeating demons. At His command the demons fled and the man was totally delivered.

3. His healing of a demonized boy (Read Mark 9:14-32). This story again demonstrates how Jesus openly confronted and defeated demonic powers. As before, the demons had to obey His command.

Jesus, of course, did many other signs, wonders, and miracles throughout His ministry. Space, however, does not allow us to look at all of them. Each time he combined proclamation of the gospel with a demonstration of God's power.

In the Teachings of His Disciples

Not only did Jesus come to destroy the works of the devil Himself, He taught His disciples to do the same. His ministry was a pattern for theirs—and for our ministries today.

Twice Jesus sent His disciples out on training missions (Luke 9:1-6; 10:1-23). On the second mission, after the Seventy-two reported back to Him, Jesus reminded them of the authority He had given them to "overcome all the power of the enemy" (10:19). A bit later, He gave His disciples an extended teaching on how deal with demonic powers (Luke 11:14-26).

In the Passing on of His Ministry

Jesus passed on His ministry to His disciples through practical training sessions (Mark 3:14; Luke 9:1-2). He promised them that they could expect the same signs to follow their ministries as followed His (Mark 16:15-20). Jesus' final and most dramatic act of passing on His ministry of power to His followers took place on the Day of Pentecost. On that day He gave to them the same power that had enabled Him in His ministry (Luke 4:17-18; Acts 10:38). This happened when they were all filled with the Holy Spirit (Acts 1:8; 2:4). This same Pentecostal power is available to us today (John 14:26; 16:7).

POWER ENCOUNTER IN THE MINISTRY
OF THE EARLY CHURCH

Having received power of the Spirit on the day of Pentecost, the early disciples went out and ministered as Jesus had taught them. They not only declared the gospel, they demonstrated that the kingdom of God had come in great power.

Observations About the Early Church

The ministry of the church in the book of Acts was a continuation of the ministry of the Holy Spirit who had anointed and empowered Jesus (Acts 1:1). In addition to powerful proclamation of the gospel, the apostles' ministry included various supernatural signs. Often, as a result of a demonstration of God's power, wonder and amazement came upon the people. The gospel was then preached and thousands were saved. The same can happen today if we, like the early church, will follow the twofold pattern set by Jesus.

Examples of Power Encounter in the Early Church

In the following exercise you can examine a couple of examples of power ministry in Acts for yourself. First read the assigned passage, then answer the four questions.

1. The Day of Pentecost. Carefully read Acts 2:1-41 and answer the following questions:
- What demonstrations of God's power took place on the Day of Pentecost?
- What was the reaction of the crowd to these demonstrations of power?
- Does a truth encounter also occur? If so, briefly describe it.
- What are the results of this power encounter?

2. Healing at the Beautiful Gate. Carefully read Acts 3:1-26. Answer the same four questions as you did in the previous example:
- What demonstration of God's power took place at the Beautiful Gate?
- What was the reaction of the crowd to this demonstration of power?
- Does a truth encounter also occur? If so, briefly describe it.
- What are the results of this power encounter?

Class Discussion

Discuss the following in class:
1. Why do we say that the ten plagues upon Egypt and Elijah's contest against the prophets of Baal are power encounters?
2. Why are both power encounter and truth encounter necessary in our evangelistic and church-planting efforts today?

Power Encounter and the Kingdom of God

Central Truth
An understanding of the kingdom of God is essential to an effective power ministry.

Lesson Outline
- The Kingdom of God Defined
- The Coming of the Kingdom of God
- Preaching the Kingdom of God

Introduction
The kingdom of God is one of the most important themes of the Bible. In the four gospels Jesus spoke of the kingdom of God, or its equivalent, the kingdom of heaven, more than 90 times. This lesson will address this important subject.

THE KINGDOM OF GOD DEFINED

We should not think of the kingdom of God as a place or a geographical region. It is, rather, the rule or a reign of God. It speaks of God's sovereign authority over His creation.

Two Tenses of the Kingdom
The kingdom of God has both a present and a future tense. The Kingdom has come, but it is also coming. It is really here, but it is not fully here. Let's look more closely at these two tenses of the Kingdom:

1. The kingdom of God is already present. The overthrow of Satan's kingdom has already begun, and the power of the Age to Come is already at work in the world today. It came in the person and through the work of Jesus Christ (Luke 17:20-21). It came again on the Day of Pentecost when Jesus transferred His kingdom ministry and His kingdom power to His church (Mark 9:1; Acts 1:8).

2. The kingdom of God is coming. While the invasion of Satan's kingdom has begun, there remains a future establishing of Christ's sovereign rule. The kingdom of God will come in fullness at the second coming of Christ (Rev. 11:15).

This truth—that the Kingdom has come and is yet coming— helps us to understand our present experience. It explains our triumph over Satan on one hand, and our continuing warfare with him on the other. It explains why many today are dramatically healed, and yet others remain sick and die. It explains why we have power over demons, and yet Satan continues to exercise control over many people and many areas of our world. The kingdom of God has come in part; someday it will come in completeness. Now we have power and authority over demons, but then all the powers of darkness will be completely and finally defeated.

THE COMING OF THE KINGDOM OF GOD

Jesus came to announce the rule and reign of God. It was the central theme of His preaching (Matt. 4:23; Mark 1:14-15; Luke 8:1, 9:11). He once said, "I must preach the good news of the kingdom of God...because that is why I was sent" (Luke 4:43). He began His ministry by saying, "The time has come...the kingdom of God is near" (Mark 1:15). Jesus was saying that the kingdom of God had arrived, and was now within reach of anyone who would take hold of it.

The kingdom of God was also the central theme of the preaching of Christ's disciples. When Jesus sent them out to minister, He instructed them to proclaim the Kingdom and to demonstrate its power (Matt. 10:7; Luke 9:2; 10:9-11).

The Coming of God's Kingdom Results in Conflict

The kingdom of God is now forcefully advancing through the church empowered by the Holy Spirit. Because Satan, the usurper, is strongly opposing the coming of the Kingdom, confrontation results. As a result, a violent spiritual war has broken out (Eph. 6:12).

The Coming of God's Kingdom is with Power

God's kingdom comes in power (1 Cor. 4:20). In fact, it can come in no other way. Because of Satan's stubborn resistance to the coming of the Kingdom, it must advance in power. The supplanter must be evicted by force (Matt. 12:28-29).

Thus, the church, if it is to effectively advance Christ's kingdom in the earth, must move in the power of the Spirit. Once Jesus told His disciples, "I tell you the truth, some who are standing here will not taste death before they see the kingdom of God come with power" (Mark 9:1). He was speaking of the Day of Pentecost, when His church would be clothed with power from on high (Luke 24:49). Today, the kingdom of God comes in power each time someone filled with or touched by the Spirit of God (Acts 1:8).

Signs of the Coming Kingdom

Signs, wonders, and miracles show that the kingdom of God is present. They are a foreshadowing of what life will be like when the kingdom of God has come in its fullness. Healing today is a foreshadowing of the ending of all suffering and sickness (Rev. 21:4). Casting out of demons signals God's invasion of the realm of Satan, and foreshadows his final destruction when Jesus returns (Rev. 20:10).

Jesus taught us to pray "Your kingdom come" (Matt. 6:10). In doing this He was instructing us to pray for at least three things:

1. For people to be saved. The kingdom of God comes personally to an individual when he or she is born again (Luke 17:21; John 3:5).

2. For people to be filled with the Spirit, healed, and delivered from demonic affliction. The kingdom of God comes in power when people are empowered by the Spirit or set free by the power of God (Luke 11:20; compare 10:9).

3. For Jesus to come again (Rev. 22:20). When Jesus comes again He will defeat Satan and establish His sovereign reign in the earth. Then the kingdom of God will have come in its fullness.

PREACHING THE KINGDOM OF GOD

Jesus sent out His disciples to announce that God, through Christ, had come to set up His reign on earth (Matt. 10:7). When He sent out the Twelve He told them to "preach the kingdom of God and to heal the sick" (Luke 9:1-2). To the Seventy-two He said, "Heal the sick who are there and tell them, 'The kingdom of God is near you'" (10:9). Further, during the forty days following His resurrection, Jesus spoke much about the kingdom of God (Acts 1:3).

One important kingdom topic Jesus discussed was the necessity of being filled with the Spirit in order to be His witnesses to the ends of the earth (Acts 1:4-8). The preaching of the Kingdom continued throughout the book of Acts (8:5-6; 12; 19:8; 20:25; 28:30). We, too, have been called to proclaim the gospel of the kingdom until Jesus comes again (Matt. 24:14).

The Gospel of the Kingdom of Defined

What then is this gospel of the kingdom that Jesus has commissioned us to proclaim? It is the good news that the King has come, and that He has defeated His enemies and the enemies of mankind at the cross and through His glorious resurrection from the dead. Someone describe the gospel of the kingdom as the gospel of salvation with the addition of the powers of the Age to Come.

Jesus and the early church not only announced the coming of God's kingdom and the overthrow of Satan's kingdom, they demonstrated the powers of the Kingdom by healing the sick, driving out demons, and other demonstrations of the Spirit's power. Jesus said, "From the days of John the Baptist until now, the kingdom of heaven has been forcefully advancing, and forceful men lay hold of it" (Matt. 11:12).

We are not only to be proclaimers of Jesus' message, we are to be imitators of His methods and demonstrators of His kingdom power. As representatives of God's kingdom we have been called by God and anointed by the Spirit to minister as Jesus ministered.

Class Discussion

Discuss the following in class:
1. Discuss the two tenses of the Kingdom. How will a proper understanding of these concepts affect the way we preach the gospel?
2. Why does the coming of the kingdom of God result in conflict? How does this truth affect how we should minister today?
3. Why is it important that we be filled with the Spirit as we seek to advance the kingdom of God?
4. How will this new understanding of the kingdom of God influence the way you minister in the future?

Power Encounter and Preaching the Gospel

Central Truth
Our preaching and teaching must contain the two essential elements of true gospel witness: proclamation and demonstration.

Lesson Outline
* Two Essential Elements of Gospel Witness
* Power Encounter in the Teaching and Preaching of Jesus and the Early Church

Introduction
In our last lesson we talked about preaching the gospel of the kingdom of God. In this lesson we will expand on the subject of preaching the gospel and how it relates to power ministry.

TWO ESSENTIAL ELEMENTS OF GOSPEL WITNESS

Two essential elements of true gospel witness are proclamation and demonstration. The truth of the gospel must be proclaimed and its power must be demonstrated. Proclamation is the preaching of the gospel. Demonstration is the anointing, signs, wonders, and miracles that accompany our preaching.

Getting First Things First
Jesus taught us that we must often do spiritual battle before the gospel can be effectively proclaimed. He said, "If I drive out demons by the Spirit of God, then the kingdom of God has come upon you. Or again, how can anyone enter a strong man's house and carry off his possessions unless he *first* ties up the strong man? *Then* he can rob his house" (Matt. 12:28-20, emphasis added). Jesus was teaching about the importance of getting first things first in preaching the gospel. Many times we must *first* "tie up the strong man," *then* we can "rob his house." The first sign Jesus promised to those fulfilling His Great Commission is that "they will drive out demons" (Mark 16:17). Many times our first order of business is to overpower the

demonic forces. Only then can we effectively proclaim liberty and salvation to those held hostage.

Power plus

As we have already noted, Christ has given us all the tools we need to complete the job. As you may remember, two of those tools are the power of the Holy Spirit and the power of the gospel. The unfailing formula for effective gospel witness is

The Power of the Holy Spirit + The Power of the Gospel = Amazing Results.

Let's briefly examine each part of this formula:

1. The power of the Holy Spirit. Jesus promised supernatural power to all who receive the Holy Spirit (Acts 1:8). It is, therefore, essential that everyone involved in sharing the gospel with others be filled with the Spirit. Further, he or she must know how to release the power of the Holy Spirit in ministry.

2. Plus the power of the gospel. The seed of the gospel contains within itself miraculous reproductive power (Mark 4:26-29). Paul described it as "the power of God for...salvation" (Rom. 1:16-17). The gospel is the message of Jesus and all that He has done, all that He is doing, and all that He will do in the future. At the heart of the gospel is the message of His death, burial, and resurrection (1 Cor. 15:1-4). We must never fail to preach this powerful message.

3. Equals amazing results. If we will faithfully combine these two elements—the power of the Holy Spirit and the power of the gospel—we can expect amazing results. This is what happened in the early church in the book of Acts.

POWER ENCOUNTER IN THE PREACHING AND TEACHING OF JESUS AND THE EARLY CHURCH

Both Jesus and the early church preached the gospel in the power of the Holy Spirit with signs following. Let's look briefly at each:

The Preaching and Teaching of Jesus

In His own ministry Jesus preached the gospel and demonstrated the power of the Holy Spirit (Matt. 4:23; 9:35). This resulted in large crowds coming to hear His message and following Him (Mark 4:24-25; 9:36). When He commissioned and later sent out the Twelve and the Seventy-two (Mark 3:13-15; Luke 9:1-2; 10:1-16), Jesus gave them authority to drive out demons, heal the sick, and preach the gospel of the kingdom (10:9). Later, when He commissioned His church to preach the gospel in all the world, He promised them supernatural power (Mark 15:17-18; Luke 24:48-49; John 20:21-22). This power comes when one is filled with the Holy Spirit (Acts 1:8).

The Preaching and Teaching of the Early Church

Throughout Acts the early church repeatedly combined the preaching of the gospel with a demonstration of the Spirit's power. Because of space we will cite only three representative examples:

1. The Day of Pentecost. (Read Acts 2:1-41.) On the Day of Pentecost the Jewish pilgrims who entered the Temple courts had no interest in hearing Peter preach the gospel. However, after they saw the demonstrations of God's power—the wind, fire, and tongues—a great "faith shift" took place in their hearts. They were suddenly ready to hear and believe the gospel. When Peter stood to preach, they listened closely to what he said. And when he completed his sermon, 3000 readily responded to the call for salvation.

2. The Beautiful Gate. (Read Acts 3:1–4:4.) At the Beautiful Gate the disciples followed the same pattern of combining a demonstration God's power with a clear presentation of the gospel. As a result of the lame man's healing, the previously disinterested crowd was "filled with wonder and amazement" and came running to the disciples. Again, Peter delivered a Christ-centered message, and many believed and followed Christ.

3. The Ministry of Philip. (Read Acts 8:1-7.) This same pattern is again seen in the ministry of Philip. In the city of Samaria he preached Christ and demonstrated God's power through miraculous signs. As a result, the people listened closely to what he said and believed the gospel as he preached. The outcome was "great joy in the city" (v. 8).

If we are to see the same dramatic results today as did these New Testament evangelists, we must follow the same pattern they followed—proclamation combined with demonstration.

In the Letters of Paul

The same pattern of demonstration plus proclamation is clearly taught in the letters of Paul. Let's look at three examples:

1. 1 Corinthians 2:2-5. In this passage Paul reminds the Corinthians how he preached the gospel to them: "I resolved to know nothing while I was with you except Jesus Christ and him crucified... My message and my preaching were...with a demonstration of the Spirit's power." Note how Paul's ministry in Corinth had two emphases: the message of "Jesus Christ and him crucified," and a "demonstration of the Spirit's power."

2. Romans 15:18-20. When describing his apostolic ministry to the Romans, Paul tells them that it consisted of both what he *said* and what he *did*. He performed "signs and miracles, through the power of the Spirit," and he "fully proclaimed the gospel of Christ."

3. 1 Thessalonians 1:5. In this verse Paul reminded the Thessalonians of how the gospel came to them: "not simply with words, but also with power, with the Holy Spirit, and with deep conviction."

In this lesson we have shown that there are two important elements in a true witness of the gospel of Christ. One is a clear presentation of the gospel, the other is a demonstration of the Spirit's power. If our witness is to be as effective as that of Jesus and the apostles, we must learn to use both of these methods.

Class Discussion
Discuss the following in class:
1. We must often challenge the powers of darkness before we can effectively preach the gospel in certain areas? Why is this important?
2. Describe the "faith shift" that takes place in people's hearts when they see a demonstration of God's power.
3. Read Romans 15:18-20. How does Paul describe the two emphases of his apostolic ministry?

Preparation for a Power Ministry

Central Truth
Anyone wanting to be involved in power evangelism must give serious attention to his or her own personal resources and preparation.

Lesson Outline
- Essential Elements of a Power Ministry
- Preparation for Power Ministry

Introduction
In this lesson we will answer two questions about power ministry: (1) What are the essential elements of a power ministry? and (2) What personal preparation is necessary for such a ministry?

ESSENTIAL ELEMENTS OF A POWER MINISTRY

At least five elements go into the development of an effective power ministry. Let's examine each of these elements:

Anointing
Anointing is the manifest presence of the Holy Spirit that comes upon a Spirit-filled Christian as he or she is involved in ministry. It is sometimes called God's "manifest presence." Let's look at four examples in Acts of the Spirit anointing individuals to do ministry:

1. Peter. An anointing of the Spirit came upon Peter when he and John were called before the Jewish Sanhedrin to explain their healing of a crippled man, and their of preaching the gospel in the Temple court. (Read and discuss Acts 4:5-12.)

2. The apostles. After being refilled with the Spirit, the apostles ministered under a powerful anointing of the Holy Spirit. (Read and discuss Acts 4:31-33.)

3. Stephen. Stephen, "a man full of faith and the Holy Spirit," was so anointed by the Spirit that, as he ministered, the people "saw Stephen's face become as radiant as an angel's" (Acts 6:15, Living Bible). (Read and discuss Acts 6:5-10, 15, 55-56.)

4. Paul. An anointing of the Holy Spirit came upon Paul as he ministered on the island of Cyprus, revealing to him the judgment of God that was to immediately come upon the sorcerer, Elymas. (Read and discuss Acts 13:9-11.)

Today, if one expects to minister in the power of the Spirit as did these early Christians, he or she must learn to walk in the Spirit and be ready to yield themselves to the Spirit's promptings and control—that is, His anointing—as the He directs.

Faith

Faith is another essential element of power ministry. Faith is confidence that Christ is who He says He is, and that He will do what He says He will do. Such faith enthusiastically looks to God to confirm His word. It is seen in the eagerness of Peter and John when they told the lame man to "Look at us!" (Acts 3:4). They had something he needed, and they were anxious to give it away!

Boldness

Boldness is the willingness to take the risk of faith, even when taking such a risk could result in failure and embarrassment. Such boldness is illustrated in the ministry of Paul, when in Lystra he commanded the lame man to "Stand up on your feet!" (Acts 14:10). If the man had not walked, Paul would have been humiliated, and his ministry in Lystra would have ended. However, Paul was bold in faith, willing to risk failure. As a result the man was healed, and a mighty revival broke out in the city. Success in power ministry will come only to those who are willing to act in boldness and faith.

Divine Guidance

Before one can minister in power in any given situation, he or she must first discern the will of God in the matter, for God will never act outside of His will. The Spirit-filled worker must continually ask, "What is God's will in this matter? How does He want to move? How may I align myself with His will?" Jesus is our example in ministry. He never ministered on His own initiative, but always followed the leading of His heavenly Father (John 5:19-20; 8:28; 12:49-50).

Humility

Humility is the ability to see ourselves as God sees us, that is, to see ourselves as we really are (see Rom. 12:3). Such an attitude is essential to a successful and enduring power ministry. We must never forget that all the power is God's, and so is the glory.

PREPARATION FOR POWER MINISTRY

How may one prepare himself or herself for a power ministry? If you sincerely wants to be used by God in a ministry of power, you must address five critical issues:

Check Your Motives

What we do for God is very important; *why* we do it is even more important. We must each carefully examine our motives for wanting to be used by God in a ministry of power evangelism. Wrong motives include pride, desire for personal gain and advancement, and the need to exercise control over people. Right motives include a desire to glorify God, a love for and a desire to help people, and a desire to advance God's kingdom in the earth.

Strengthen Your Relationship

Just as Jesus ministered out His relationship with His heavenly Father (John 5:20), we, too, minister out of our relationship with God. Our ministry *for* God will never be stronger than our bond *with* Him.

In like manner, the apostles ministered out of their relationship with Christ (Acts 4:13). Anyone wanting to be used by God in a ministry of power evangelism must, like Jesus and the apostles, spend much time in secret prayer, strengthening their relationship with God.

Increase Your Understanding

A third way to prepare oneself for ministry in the supernatural is to increase his or her understanding of the subject. Learning and applying the principles in this study is a good first step. Another way is by reading and rereading the gospels and Acts. As you read, ask such questions as, "How did Jesus and the apostles minister in power? How did they heal the sick and cast out devils? What were the secrets of their success? How may I imitate their lives and ministries?" You may also read books on the subject by reputable men and women of God.

Submit to God's Will

Jesus submitted Himself absolutely to the will of His heavenly Father, and thus received his Father's blessing. We too, if we are to receive the blessing of God, must submit ourselves totally to His will. We must never forget: God will only anoint *His* plans, and He has promised only to confirm *His* Word, not ours, with signs following (Mark 16:15-20).

Get Experience

Finally, if one intends to be involved in a ministry of power, he or she must acquire the necessary experience. This includes both spiritual and practical experience.

1. Spiritual experience. Spiritual experience must include being born again (John 3:3-7). Also, one must be filled with the Spirit as were the first-century disciples (Acts 1:8; 2:4). The baptism in the Holy Spirit was the early church's source of spiritual dynamic and power, and it remains our source of spiritual power today (2:38-39).

2. Practical experience. As with any other job, competence in power ministry is gained through practice. The person wanting to become competent in this area of ministry must do so through practical experience. This experience is best gained in working with an experienced minister. This is how the Twelve, under the guidance of Jesus, gained practical experience. As we participate in power ministry, we will experience both successes and failures. In this way we will learn to more effectively minister for Christ.

In summary, anyone desiring to be used in power ministry must give serious attention to his or her own personal preparation. He or she must never forget that we minister, not out of our own strength and resources, but out of the strength and resources of God.

Class Discussion

Discuss the following in class:
1. What is meant by the phrase "the anointing?" What phrases are used to describe the anointing in the Scripture texts presented in this lesson?
2. Explain why boldness is essential in a power ministry.
3. Why is divine guidance so necessary in power ministry?
4. Why is it important that the one who wants to be used in a ministry of power strengthen his or her relationship with God?

The Baptism in the Holy Spirit and Power Encounter

Central Truth
Before one can be truly effective in power ministry, he or she must understand and experience the baptism in the Holy Spirit.

Lesson Outline
- The Baptism in the Holy Spirit Defined
- The Importance of the Baptism in the Holy Spirit to a Power Ministry
- How To Receive the Holy Spirit Today

Introduction
The baptism in the Holy Spirit is an experience for all believers and it is our source of spiritual power for life and ministry. In this lesson we will examine this vital Christian experience.

THE BAPTISM IN THE HOLY SPIRIT DEFINED

The baptism in the Holy can be described in many ways. By way of definition, we will mention four:

Both an Immersion and a Filling
Both John the Baptist and Jesus promised a baptism (or immersion) in the Holy Spirit (Luke 3:16; Acts 1:4-5). On the Day of Pentecost, when the promise was first fulfilled, the disciples were "all filled with the Holy Spirit" (Acts 2:4). Just as an opened container can, at the same time, be both immersed in and filled with water, so it is with those who are baptized in the Holy Spirit.

Separate from Regeneration
The baptism in the Holy Spirit is an experience separate and distinct from the new birth. Just as the Samaritans (Acts 8:12-14), Paul (9:3-18), and the Ephesians (19:1-7) were first born again, and later "received the Holy Spirit" (Acts 8:17), so it can be with believers today.

A Clothing with Power

Jesus described the baptism in the Holy Spirit as a clothing with power from on high (Luke 24:49). The picture is of one being totally wrapped in, and overwhelmed by, the power of God. God gives us His power to equip us to be effective witnesses (Acts 1:8).

A Promise for All Believers

Every believer can, and should, be baptized in the Holy Spirit. On the Day of Pentecost "they were *all* filled with the Holy Spirit" (Acts 2:4). That same day Peter declared, "The promise is for you and your children and for *all* who are far off—for *all* whom the Lord our God will call" (Acts 2:39). The promise is for all of God's children. (See also Num. 11:29; Joel 2:28-29; Acts 2:17-18; 4:31; 10:44.)

THE IMPORTANCE OF THE BAPTISM IN THE HOLY SPIRIT TO A POWER MINISTRY

The importance of one's being baptized in the Holy Spirit before attempting a power ministry is demonstrated in at least two ways:

Commanded in Scripture

In His final message to His disciples Jesus commanded them to wait for the Spirit (Acts 1:4-5). They were not to begin their ministries until they had first received power from on high (Luke 24:49; Acts 1:8). They needed God's power to do the work to which Christ had called them. In like manner, Paul commanded believers to be filled with the Spirit (Eph. 5:18). The same is true today. Before we attempt to enter into ministry we too must be filled with the Holy Spirit.

Our Source of Power

As it was for Jesus and the early church, the Holy Spirit is our source of power for ministry today. Jesus did not begin His messianic ministry until He was first anointed by the Holy Spirit (Luke 3:21-23; 4:17-19; Acts 10:38). After His anointing, He at once began to minister in the Spirit's power. (Read and discuss Luke 3:22-23; 4:1-2; 4:14; 18-21; 5:17; 6:19.) The same was true for the early believers. They did not begin their ministries until they were first baptized in the Holy Spirit (Acts 2:4ff). Once they were filled with the Spirit, they went out and ministered in great power and effectiveness (Acts 4:33).

On several occasions in Acts people were baptized in, or filled with, the Spirit (Acts 2:4; 4:8, 31-33; 8:17; 9:17, 18; 10:44-46; 19:6). Dramatic demonstrations of God's power and powerful anointed preaching followed each of these outpourings. As a result, a great many people came to the Lord. The same power is available to us today if we, like them, will be empowered by the Spirit.

HOW TO RECEIVE THE HOLY SPIRIT TODAY

How can one be baptized in the Holy Spirit today? We will now answer this important question. It is our hope that after reading these instructions you will personally receive this promised gift.

Preconditions for Receiving
There are two preconditions for being baptized in the Holy Spirit: First, one must be truly born again (John 14:17). Only those who have truly repented of their sins can receive the gift of the Holy Spirit (Acts 2:38-39). Next, one must desire God more than anything else in the world (John 7:37). Jesus said, "Blessed are those who hunger and thirst after righteousness, for they will be filled" (Matt. 5:6).

How to Receive the Spirit
If you will be filled with the Holy Spirit, do the following:
1. Approach the "throne of grace" with boldness. When you come to be filled with the Spirit, come confidently before God (Heb 4:16). We can come before God without fear because we know we are acting in accordance with His perfect will (1 John 5:14).
2. Ask God to fill you with the Holy Spirit. Jesus promised, "Your Father in heaven [will] give the Holy Spirit to those who ask him!" (Read and discuss Luke 11:9-13.) Just ask Him; the Lord is ready now to fill you with His Spirit.
3. Receive by faith. The baptism in the Holy Spirit is received by faith (Gal. 3:14). This, however, is not a passive faith that sits and waits on God to move. It is an aggressive faith that reaches out and takes what God has graciously offered. Jesus gave us the key for receiving the Holy Spirit when He said, "Therefore I tell you, whatever you ask for in prayer, believe that you have received it, and it will be yours" (Mark 11:24). Ask God for the Holy Spirit, expecting Him to immediately fill you. Then, by a bold act of faith, believe that you *have* received. The instant you believe, the Spirit will come and fill you. You will sense His Presence deep within.

4. Speak in faith. Once you sense the Spirit's presence deep inside, speak! Not from your mind, but from your spirit, that is, from your "innermost being," where you feel His presence (see 1 Cor. 14:14-15). As you speak out in faith, and as you yield yourself completely to God, you will begin to speak in tongues as the Spirit gives the words (Acts 2:4; 10:46; 19:6). As Jesus promised, "rivers of living water" will flow from your innermost being (John 7:38).

Evidences of Receiving
Once you have been filled with the Spirit, you will never be the same. You can expect certain "evidences" to follow your infilling:

1. The initial evidence. The first evidence of your receiving the Holy Spirit will be speaking in other tongues as the Spirit enables you. This was the recurring evidence experienced by believers in the book of Acts (2:1-4; 10:45-47; 19:1-6). Speaking in tongues is a sign from God that He has empowered you to be His witness (Acts 1:8; 2:4).

2. Other scriptural evidences. As you learn to walk in the Spirit many other evidences will follow. Some that apply directly to ministry in the Spirit are power to witness (Acts 1:8), boldness (Acts 2:14-41; 4:31), power to do the works of Jesus (John 14:16-18; 16:14), the manifestation spiritual gifts (1 Cor. 12:1-11), and a greater desire and ability to pray and to intercede for others (Rom. 8:28-29).

The power of the Spirit is essential to any power ministry. This power is given when one is baptized in the Holy Spirit. It is essential, therefore, that anyone wanting to be used by God in the area of power evangelism be baptized in the Holy Spirit. If you have not been baptized in the Holy Spirit, you should immediately seek to be filled. Right now, ask God to fill you with His Spirit.

Class Discussion
Discuss the following in class:
1. Why do we say that it is necessary for every believer to be baptized in the Holy Spirit?
2. What must one do to be filled with the Holy Spirit?
3. Discuss reasons why some believers are not filled with the Spirit today. How can each of these reasons be overcome?

– Lesson 7 –
Gifts of the Holy Spirit and Power Encounter

Central Truth
Anyone wanting to be used in power ministry must know how to release spiritual gifts in ministry.

Lesson Outline
* Spiritual Gifts Defined
* Spiritual Gifts and Power Encounter
* Releasing Spiritual Gifts

It is primarily through the gifts of the Holy Spirit that the power received at Spirit baptism is released in ministry. Therefore, anyone wanting to be used in a ministry of power must know how these gifts, especially the nine "manifestation gifts" of 1 Corinthians 12:8-10, operate in the life of a Spirit-filled believer. This lesson will address this important issue.

SPIRITUAL GIFTS DEFINED

Gifts Defined
Spiritual gifts have been defined many ways. For this study we will define spiritual gifts as *supernatural anointings released through Spirit-filled believers by the Holy Spirit to accomplish the will of the Father.*

Gifts Explained
Let's examine each part of the above definition:

1. Supernatural anointings. Spiritual gifts come as "anointings." They are administered under the impulse and direction of the Holy Spirit.

2. Released through Spirit-filled believers. Gifts are *released* as the Spirit moves upon, and through, a yielded believer. Being gifts, they are dispensed, not on the basis of merit or reward, but as simple demonstrations of God's grace. They are not, however, given as personal possessions, but are released through yielded believers on a case-by-case basis to meet specific needs in relation to God's work.

3. By the Holy Spirit. The gifts are dispensed by Holy Spirit (1 Cor. 12:4-6). They therefore operate, not according to the will of man, but according to the will of the Spirit (1 Cor. 12:11).

4. To accomplish the will of the Father. The gifts are not given to fulfill the plans and desires of any person. They are given to accomplish God's will, build up the church, and to advance His kingdom in the earth.

Spiritual Gifts Identified

Let's look more closely at the nine "manifestations" (Greek: *phanerosis*) of the Spirit listed in 1 Corinthians 12:

> Now to each one the manifestation of the Spirit is given for the common good. To one there is given through the Spirit the *message of wisdom,* to another the *message of knowledge* by means of the same Spirit, to another *faith* by the same Spirit, to another *gifts of healing* by that one Spirit, to another *miraculous powers,* to another *prophecy,* to another *distinguishing between spirits,* to another *speaking in different kinds of tongues,* and to still another *the interpretation of tongues.* (vv. 7-10, emphasis added)

These nine gifts seem to fall naturally into three groupings. The first grouping we call "revelation gifts." These revelation gifts are given *that we might know the mind of God.* They are the word of knowledge, the word of wisdom, and the discerning of spirits. The second grouping we call "prophetic gifts." These are given *that we might speak the words of God.* They include the gift of prophecy, the gift of tongues, and the interpretation of tongues. The third grouping we call "power gifts." These are given *that we might do the works of God.* These are gifts of healings, the gift of faith, and miraculous powers (or works of power). (For definitions of these gifts see Appendix 1, page 55.)

SPIRITUAL GIFTS AND POWER ENCOUNTER

How do each of these three groupings of gifts relate to a power ministry?

Revelation Gifts and Power Encounter

In Acts a word of knowledge or a discerning of spirits often began a chain of events leading to the release of a power gift (see Acts 3:1-8; 14:8-10; 16:16-18). Before one can do the work of God, he or she must first know the will of God concerning a given matter. Before Jesus healed the sick He first heard from His heavenly Father, then He did as the Father directed (John 5:19). Likewise, it is essential that we discern God's will before proceeding in ministry. Such revelation is often received through the revelation gifts.

Also, it is often crucial that the gift of discerning of spirits be exercised before we can know how to approach a healing encounter. We must determine not only *how* a person is sick, but *why* he or she is sick. Is the sickness caused by natural causes or by demonic affliction? The revelation gifts often set the stage for the release of power gifts.

Prophetic Gifts and Power Encounter

A prophetic gift will often precede or follow a demonstration of God's power. On the Day of Pentecost, after God had demonstrated His awesome power, Peter preached a powerful anointed message (Acts 2:14-36). As a result of seeing and hearing the miracles of Pentecost (power encounter), and hearing the prophetic utterance of Peter (truth encounter), the people were deeply convicted of their sins (Acts 2:37) and 3,000 were saved and baptized that very day (v. 41).

Power Gifts and Power Encounter

Power gifts represent the most obvious use of the gifts of the Spirit in power evangelism. Through the release of the gifts of healing, miraculous power, and faith, people are healed, God's power and presence are demonstrated, sinners are brought face to face with the reality of a living God, and hearts are prepared to receive the gospel.

RELEASING SPIRITUAL GIFTS

How may one be used in the gifts of the Holy Spirit? The Christian worker must to learn to walk in the Spirit and to yield to the Spirit as He prompts. With this in mind, we will address two important questions concerning the release of the spiritual gifts in ministry:

How the Anointing Comes

God anoints us and gives us His Spirit as we walk in obedience to Him. This is also true in ministering spiritual gifts. When the Holy Spirit prompts us to speak a prophetic word or to minister healing to a sick person, we must obey His voice. As we obey and begin to minister, God sends His Spirit to fill and anoint us, enabling us to do that ministry. He will release through us the gift, or gifts, needed to accomplish the work. If, however, we refuse to obey His voice, and ignore the Spirit's promptings, the anointing will not come. The principle is this: the anointing comes a the point of obedience.

How the Anointing Is Released

Once the anointing comes, the spiritual gift must then be released by an act of faith. Just as a switch releases the potential energy in the electrical wires, faith releases the anointing to accomplish the work of God. This is what happened to Peter at the Beautiful Gate. He acted in bold faith by commanding the lame man to walk and taking him by the hand and lifting him up (Acts 3:6). At that instant, a gift of healing was released and the man was healed. The same thing happened to Paul when he commanded the lame man in Lystra to stand up (Acts 14:9).

When the Holy Spirit wants a work to be done, He will often direct a Spirit-filled disciple to do it. As the disciple obeys, the Holy Spirit comes upon him and fills him. Then, as the Spirit prompts, the disciple must act in bold faith. When the disciple acts, the anointing is released, the gift is manifested, and the work is accomplished.

Gifts of the Spirit are enablements God has given to us that He may work His works through us. They are essential equipment for power ministry. We must each make it our aim to understand these powerful manifestations of the Holy Spirit, and we must know how to release them in ministry.

Class Discussion

Discuss the following in class:
1. What do we mean when we say spiritual gifts are "supernatural anointings?"
2. What is the purpose of spiritual gifts?
3. How are spiritual gifts released in ministry? What is the role of obedience? What is the role faith?

Divine Guidance and Power Encounter

Central Truth
If one is to be effective in power ministry, he or she must learn to hear and properly respond to the voice of the Spirit.

Lesson Outline
- The Importance of Divine Guidance in Power Ministry
- Hearing the Voice of God

Introduction
In this lesson we will address the issue of divine guidance and power ministry.

THE IMPORTANCE OF DIVINE GUIDANCE IN POWER MINISTRY

Important in the Ministry of Jesus
Every act of Jesus' ministry was done under the direct supervision of His heavenly Father through the Holy Spirit. He only did what the Father told Him to do. Sometimes Jesus would heal all who were sick in a place (Matt. 4:23-24; 8:16). At other times he would heal only one, as at the Pool of Bethesda (John 5:1-8). But why did Jesus heal only one man at Bethesda? Jesus told us why: "The Son can do nothing by himself; he can do only what he sees his Father doing" (vv. 19). Here is an important key to a successful power ministry. We who desire to be used by God must learn to hear and respond to the voice of the Spirit.

Important in the Ministry of the Early Church
The apostles learned how to minister by watching and imitating the ministry of Jesus. Like Him, they constantly sought and received divine guidance in the performance of their ministries.

Jesus and the apostles often witnessed by "divine appointment." God often set up the witnessing appointment for them, and then directed them into the witnessing situation. Let's look at three New

Testament examples of individuals ministering by divine appointment:

1. Jesus and the Samaritan woman. (Read John 4:1-42.) In this story Jesus "*had* to go through Samaria" (v. 4). But why? Because His heavenly Father had set up a divine appointment for Him there. There was a woman who needed Him, and a town ready to receive the gospel.

2. Philip and the Ethiopian eunuch. (Read Acts 8:26-40.) Philip was sent by the Spirit to Gaza because God had arranged a divine appointment for him with an African man hungry to know the living God. As you read this story, notice how God arranged every circumstance so that the man was ready to hear the message of Christ.

3. Peter and the household of Cornelius. (Read Acts 10:1-48.) God arranged a meeting between Peter and the Roman centurion. Having set up the meeting, the Spirit directed both men through visions (vv. 3-4, 10-11) and by speaking directly to Peter (v. 19). If we, like Jesus and the apostles, are going to minister effectively, we too must learn to hear and obey the voice of God.

HEARING THE VOICE OF GOD

If you will know how to hear the voice of God, understand and apply the following principles:

Realize that God is Speaking to You

God, by His very nature, is a speaking God. Like any loving father, He delights in speaking to His children on a regular basis. In fact, He has probably been speaking to you today! If you are not hearing Him, it could be that you have never learned how to listen to Him.

Understand the Ways That God Speaks

God speaks to His children in at least four ways:

1. The primary means. God's primary means of speaking to His children is through His Word, the Holy Bible. If you want to know what God is saying to you, read your Bible. This is the only absolutely reliable means of hearing God's voice. Any other means must be weighed and judged by this primary means.

2. Dramatic means. God sometimes speaks to his children through more dramatic means, such as dreams, visions, angelic visitations, and even speaking in an audible voice. Although God at times uses such means, they are not His most common means of speaking—either today or even in the Bible. The best stance we can take concerning these dramatic means is that we should not seek them; however, if God chooses to use them, we should welcome them.

3. The most usual means. God's most usual means of speaking to His children is by His Spirit to their spirits. Paul taught that the Spirit of God speaks directly to the spirits of born again Christians (Rom. 8:14, 16). He expanded on this theme in 1 Corinthians 2:9-16 where he taught that, since believers are indwelt by the Spirit of God, they can know the thoughts of God. As God's children, we can expect to regularly hear God speaking to us by this means.

4. Confirmatory means. A final way God speaks to us is through confirmatory, or indirect, means. For example, God sometimes arranges the events of our lives to direct us and show us His will. At other times He uses other Spirit-filled believers to speak to us. He may even speak to us through prophetic utterances spoken in the context of a loving body of believers. We must be careful, however, when we feel that God may be speaking to us through others. What is spoken must be in total agreement with the Word of God. And it should only confirm what God has already spoken, or will speak, directly to our own spirits.

Prepare Your Heart to Hear God's Voice

One reason we fail to hear the voice of God when He speaks is that our hearts are not properly prepared to hear Him. Just as a radio receiver must be both plugged in and tuned in before it can receive the signal from the radio station, we, too, must be plugged in and tuned in to the Spirit before we can hear the voice of God.

We get "plugged in" when we are born again (John 3:5-8). Paul said that the new birth unites our spirit with God's (1 Cor. 6:17). When we are filled with the Spirit, we receive more power and become more sensitive to the voice of the Spirit. Once we are plugged in we must tune in to the voice of the Spirit. We tune in to God by totally committing ourselves to Him and to His perfect will for our lives. We must keep our hearts tender and open to Him (Heb. 3:6-7).

Learn How to Recognize God's Voice

Further, if we are to consistently and clearly hear God speaking, we must learn to recognize His voice (see John 10:3-4). As we practice hearing and obeying the voice of the Spirit, we learn to more clearly recognize His voice when He speaks (Heb. 5:14).

Test the "Voice" to Prove if It is Truly God's

It is also essential that we test the "voice" to determine whether or not it is really God who is speaking. The Bible tells us that there are "many kinds of voices in the world" (1 Cor. 14:10, KJV). These voices include human voices—both our own inner voice (our personal thoughts) and outer voices (other people). They also include spiritual voices, including thoughts from God or from evil spirits. We must, therefore, know how to test these voices. If they are not in total agreement with the Word of God, they should be rejected.

By Faith, Practice Obeying the Voice of God

A final principle we must understand is this: if we are to learn how to recognize the voice of God, we must, by faith, begin obeying His voice when we do hear it. As we obey and follow, we learn to better discern the voice of God.

The ability to know and the faith to obey the voice of God are essential requirements for power ministry. We should make it our aim to learn how to do both.

Class Discussion

Discuss the following in class:
1. What do we mean when we say that Jesus and the apostles often witnessed by "divine appointment?"
2. Does God speak to us today? Discuss the four means He uses.
3. Has God spoken to your recently? Share your experience with the class.
4. What do we mean when we say that we must be "plugged in" and "tuned in" before we can clearly hear the voice of God?
5. How can we test to ensure that we are really hearing the voice of God? Why is this important?

The Weapons of Our Warfare
(Part 1)

Central Truth
To be effective in power ministry we must understand and know how to use the spiritual weapons that God has give to us.

Lesson Outline
- All the Weapons in God's Armory
- The Specifics of the Whole Armor of God

Introduction
In Lesson 3 we learned that Satan is opposing the advance of God's kingdom in the world. As a result, believers are involved in a great spiritual war against the kingdom of Satan (Eph. 6:12). Happily, as Christ's disciples, we have been given the weapons we need to defeat the enemy. Paul wrote, "The weapons we fight with are not the weapons of the world. On the contrary, they have divine power to demolish strongholds" (2 Cor. 10:4). In this and the next lesson we will identify and discuss how each of these spiritual weapons may be used.

ALL THE WEAPONS IN GOD'S ARMORY

Paul instructs believers to take up "all the weapons in God's armory" (Eph. 6:11, Knox translation). We are to take up these weapons so that we can do battle against the forces of Satan.

Our Source of Strength for Battle
The apostle reminds us that our source of strength is "the Lord and in his mighty power" (v. 10). Nevertheless, in preparation for battle, we must "put on the full armor of God so that [we] can take [our] stand against the devil's schemes" (v. 11).

The Purposes of the Whole Armor of God
Further, Paul tells of two purposes for this spiritual armor: that we might stand our ground against the enemy's attacks (v. 13), and that we might not fall prey to Satan's "schemes" (v. 11). These schemes

include the devil's methods, strategies, and cunning wiles. Let's look at some of the specifics of God's armor.

THE SPECIFICS OF THE WHOLE ARMOR OF GOD

Paul used the arming of a Roman legionnaire as a means of illustrating the various items in the Christian's spiritual arsenal:

> Stand firm then, with the belt of *truth* buckled around your waist, with the breastplate of *righteousness* in place, and with your feet fitted with the *readiness* that comes from the gospel of peace. In addition to all this, take up the shield of *faith,* with which you can extinguish all the flaming arrows of the evil one. Take the helmet of *salvation* and the sword of the Spirit, which is the *word of God.* And *pray in the Spirit* on all occasions with all kinds of prayers and requests. With this in mind, be alert and always keep on praying for all the saints. (Eph. 6:14-18, emphases added)

You will notice that seven key words and phrases have been emphasized in the above passage. Each word or phrase speaks of a powerful weapon the Christian's arsenal. They represent seven ways we can arm ourselves to do spiritual battle with the devil:

Armed with Truth

First, we are to be armed with truth. To put on the belt of truth could mean two things: It could mean that we are to be armed with the Word of God, which is truth (John 17:17). It could also mean that we are to arm ourselves with truthfulness, that is, with honesty and integrity.

Against what scheme of Satan can the weapon of truth be used? It can be used against his evil lies. Remember, he is a liar, and the father of all liars (John 8:44). We can stand against his lies by proclaiming the truth of God's word and by living lives of honesty and integrity before God and men.

Armed with Righteousness

In our battles with evil we are also to be armed with righteousness. Righteousness involves both right relationship and right living. We can be truly righteous only if we are in right relationship with God through Jesus Christ. As a result of this relationship we are to live clean and holy lives. By putting on righteousness, we will be able to withstand Satan's tentacles of wickedness that have defeated so many.

Armed with Readiness
Next, we are to be armed with readiness. That is, we are to be vigilant and constantly alert for the attacks of the enemy (1 Pet. 5:8). This readiness is produced by the hearing and obeying gospel (see also, Eph. 4:15). The proclamation of the gospel alerts, prepares, and equips people for the enemy's tactics.

Armed with Faith
The faith we are to take up includes saving faith, that is, a basic trust in God's provision of salvation through the atoning work of Christ on the cross. The weapon of faith, however, goes beyond saving faith. It also includes faith that aggressively reaches out and takes what God has promised. Such faith can be used as a shield to "extinguish all the flaming arrows of the evil one" (Eph. 6:16), including unsought and unholy thoughts, desires to disobey, rebellious suggestions, lust, and fear.

Faith is also a powerful offensive weapon which the Spirit-filled believer can use to defeat the enemy. Hebrews 11 tells of men and women of old who used faith to win victories and conquer kingdoms. Through faith they "became powerful in battle and routed foreign armies" (v. 34). In fact, the entire Bible is full of stories of such people who used faith as a mighty weapon to advance the kingdom of God in the earth. We, too, must learn to use this powerful spiritual weapon.

Armed with Salvation
A fifth weapon in the Christian's arsenal is the weapon of salvation. Here, we should interpret salvation in the broadest sense. This includes, not only of salvation from sin and hell, but also of any salvation or deliverance that comes from God, including deliverance from demons, danger, sickness, and death.

Armed with the Word of God
The Word of God is one of our most powerful spiritual weapons. Paul called it the "sword of the Spirit." We arm ourselves with the Word of God by learning, memorizing, and proclaiming the message of Christ. The word of God in this passage could also be a personal "word" that we might receive from the Spirit. It could be a specific passage of Scripture that the Lord impresses on our hearts, or it could

also be a revelation from God to meet a special need, including a word of knowledge or a word of wisdom (1 Cor. 12:8).

This weapon can be used for both offensive and defensive battle. It can be used as an offensive weapon when it is preached and taught under an anointing of the Spirit. It can be used as a defensive weapon to counter Satan's attacks, as did Jesus in the wilderness (Luke 4:1-13).

Armed with Prayer in the Spirit

A final spiritual weapon mentioned in Ephesian 6 is "prayer in the Spirit" (v. 18). This means any kind of Spirit-anointed, Spirit-directed prayer. It includes intercessory prayer in tongues (compare 1 Cor. 14:14 with Rom. 6:26). Praying in the Spirit is a powerful spiritual weapon. Paul tells us to never put this weapon down (v. 18). As the spiritual warrior prays in the Spirit, many blessings follow: his mind is renewed, his spiritual life is strengthened (1 Cor. 14:4), his faith is built up (Jude 20), and he prays according to the will of God (Rom. 8:27).

In the next lesson we will continue our study of the spiritual weapons.

Class Discussion

Discuss the following in class:
1. Describe the war the church is involved in.
2. Why is it necessary to use spiritual weapons to fight this war?
3. To whom do we look as our source of strength for the battle? What must we do ourselves?
4. Why is it important that we put on the whole armor of God?
5. Share with others how you used one of the spiritual weapons named in Ephesian 6 to defeat the enemy?

The Weapons of Our Warfare
(Part 2)

Central Truth
To be effective in power ministry we must understand and know how to use the spiritual weapons that God has give to us.

Lesson Outline
• Seven More Powerful Spiritual Weapons

Introduction
In this lesson we continue our study of spiritual weapons which we began in the last lesson. We will discuss seven other powerful spiritual weapons at the disciple's disposal.

SEVEN MORE POWERFUL SPIRITUAL WEAPONS

The Weapon of Fasting
When used properly, the weapon of fasting is a powerful spiritual weapon. It is to be used along with the weapon of prayer (which was discussed in the last lesson).

Mark tells the story of a demon-possessed boy (9:9-29). In this story Jesus' disciples tried unsuccessfully to cast the demon out of the boy. When the boy's father saw Jesus coming, he ran to Him, and pleaded with Him to deliver the boy. In response Jesus commanded the demon to leave, and the boy was set free. Later, Jesus' disciples asked Him, "Why could we not cast him out?" Jesus answered them, *"This kind* can come out by nothing but prayer and fasting" (Mark 9:29 NKJV, emphasis added). *This kind* of demon still exists, and prayer with fasting is often the only means to victory over such evil spirits.

There are at least four biblical reasons we need to employ the powerful spiritual weapon of fasting:

1. to help gain audience with God (Ezra 8:23)
2. to set the captives free (Isa. 58:6)
3. to gain wisdom and understanding (Dan. 9:2-3, 21-22)

4. to find the will of God in a given matter (Acts 13:2).

Take time to look up and meditate on each of the above references. It will help you to understand how powerful the weapon of fasting is.

The Weapon of Praise

Praise is another weapon available to disciples. Great spiritual power is generated through Spirit-anointed praise. When the children of Israel shouted, the walls of a Jericho fell (Josh. 6:16-20). When the singers of Jehoshaphat began to sing and praise the beauty of God's holiness, God came on the scene and set ambushes against the enemies of Israel (2 Chron. 20:1-26). As Paul and Silas prayed and sang hymns to God at midnight in a Roman prison, the power of God was manifested: "Suddenly there was such a violent earthquake that the foundations of the prison were shaken. At once all the prison doors flew open, and everybody's chains came loose" (Acts 16:26). As we praise God, His presence and power enter into our situation (Psa. 22:3, NKJV), and our enemy is confused and routed. Praise is a powerful weapon at the believer's disposal.

The Weapon of Love

Love is another of our powerful spiritual weapons. Genuine love has amazing power in directing men and women to Christ. Some, who cannot be won by our logical arguments, or even our manifestations of power, can be won to Christ through simple demonstrations of Christian love. Saul of Tarsus was, in part, persuaded to turn to Christ because of the powerful demonstration of love he witnessed in Stephen. As the stones beat out Stephen's life, he prayed, "Lord, do not hold this sin against them" (Acts 7:60). This amazing demonstration of love had a great impact on Saul's mind and prepared him for his eventual encounter with the risen Christ on the Damascus Road. Paul tells us one way we may use this weapon of love:

> Do not repay anyone evil for evil. Be careful to do what is right in the eyes of everybody… If your enemy is hungry, feed him; if he is thirsty, give him something to drink. In doing this, you will heap burning coals on his head. Do not be overcome by evil, but overcome evil with good. (Rom. 12:17, 20-21)

Thus, evil can be overcome by good, and men and women won to Christ with the powerful weapon of love.

The Weapon of the Spirit Baptism

Jesus promised His followers power when the Holy Spirit came upon them (Acts 1:8). He was speaking about an experience He called the baptism in the Holy Spirit (v. 4). This clothing of "power from on high" is an indispensable weapon for spiritual warfare, and should be earnestly sought for and received by every believer (Luke 24:49; Acts 1:8).

The Weapons of the Gifts of the Spirit

One primary reason the spiritual gifts were given to the church is that believers might do spiritual warfare, as is discussed in Lesson 7. Through these gifts the army of God is able to receive orders and directions from its Commander-in-Chief (revelation gifts), speak powerful words from heaven (prophetic gifts), and release the power of God against the enemy (power gifts).

The Weapon of Jesus' Name

Jesus has also given to us His name as a spiritual weapon to be used against the forces of evil. All the authority of heaven stands behind Jesus' name. When we use His name as He has directed, we speak with great authority. The powers of hell must yield to that name that is above every name (Phil. 2:9-11). Jesus taught us to pray in His name:

> I tell you the truth, anyone who has faith in me will do what I have been doing. He will do even greater things than these, because I am going to the Father. And I will do whatever you ask in my name, so that the Son may bring glory to the Father. You may ask me for anything in my name, and I will do it. (John 14:12-14)

> In that day you will no longer ask me anything. I tell you the truth, my Father will give you whatever you ask in my name. Until now you have not asked for anything in my name. Ask and you will receive, and your joy will be complete (John 16:23-24).

The apostles often used the name of Jesus to heal the sick, cast out demons, and to do the works of Jesus (Acts 3:6; 9:27; 16:18). We, too, can use this powerful spiritual weapon with the same results.

The Weapon of the Gospel

The gospel, that is, the message of Christ, is a mighty spiritual weapon, as was discussed in Lesson 4. Paul called it "the power of God for the salvation of everyone who believes" (Rom. 1:16). He said that it has the power to create faith in the hearts of those who hear it preached (Rom. 10:17; see also Mark 4:26-29). As the gospel is preached, the power of God is released. What a powerful weapon is the proclamation of Christ!

God has given us many powerful spiritual weapons that we may use to confront and defeat the powers of Satan. As His spiritual warriors, we must set ourselves to learn how to effectively wield each one.

Class Discussion

Discuss the following in class:
1. Discuss four benefits of using the weapon of fasting.
2. Jesus spoke of "this kind" of demon. Does this mean that there are various kinds of demons? Give reasons for your answer. Is it important to understand this truth? Why?
3. According to Luke 24:49 and Acts 1:8 what happens to a Christian when he or she is filled with the Holy Spirit?
4. State one important reason why Christ has given spiritual gifts to His church.
5. Review the seven spiritual weapons discussed in the lesson. Share with the class how you used one of these weapons to defeat the devil.

How to Heal the Sick

Central Truth
Jesus is our model of how to be used by God in healing the sick.

Lesson Outline
• Preliminary Considerations
• How to Heal the Sick

Introduction
In this and the final three lessons of this study we will discuss the practical "how to's" of power ministry. This lesson will discuss how each of us may be used by God in healing those who are sick and afflicted.

PRELIMINARY CONSIDERATIONS

Before we discuss the particulars of how to heal the sick, we will direct our attention to three preliminary considerations:

The Healing Environment
When a Christian worker approaches a healing encounter he or she should give careful consideration to the healing environment, that is, the spiritual atmosphere surrounding a ministry encounter.

Luke spoke of such an environment attending the healing ministry of Jesus: "Great crowds of people came to hear him and to be healed of their sicknesses… And the power of the Lord was present for him to heal the sick" (Luke 5:15,17). Notice how Jesus ministered healing in an atmosphere filled with the divine Presence. Before He raised Jairus' daughter from the dead, He changed the spiritual environment by putting the unbelieving mourners out of the room (Mark 5:39-42). Peter did much the same thing when he raised Dorcas from the dead (Acts 9:40). On one occasion Jesus was hindered in His healing ministry because of an atmosphere of unbelief (Mark.6:5-6, ref. Matt.13:58). These incidents reveal two important aspects of a healing environment:

1. The manifest presence of God. The manifest presence of God is the felt or observable presence of God, such as accompanied the ministry of Jesus (Luke 5:17). Other biblical examples of the manifest presence of God are Exodus 3:1-6; 2 Chronicles 7:1-3, Luke 2:8-9, Acts 2:1-13, 4:31, and 1 Corinthians 14:22-25.

2. Expectant faith. Expectant faith is the kind of faith exhibited by the sick woman who said, "If I just touch his clothes, I will be healed" (Mark 5:28). It is the faith that is present when people anticipate a miracle from God.

Approaching a Healing Encounter

As a Christian worker approaches a healing encounter he or she should ask God for a fresh infilling of the Holy Spirit. He should remind himself of who Jesus is, what He has done, and what He has told us to do. He should also pray frequently in the Spirit, constantly listening for the Spirit's voice to direct him.

How the Anointing for Ministry Comes

Spiritual gifts are released as "anointings" of the Holy Spirit, as previously discussed. When these anointings come, the Christian worker may sense an inner surge, or a sudden infusion of power. Some testify that the anointing to heal comes with a feeling of deep compassion for the one being ministered to, or a full assurance that the work will be done (see Mark 1:41). How ever the anointing comes to you personally, you will sense in your spirit that the Spirit of God is working in the situation.

HOW TO HEAL THE SICK

It is helpful to see the healing encounter as a three-step process. Each step will seek to answer one of three questions: What is the person's real need? How will the Christian worker proceed with ministry? And, how will he or she advise this person after the ministry engagement?

Three Step Pastoral Model for Healing the Sick

Step 1: the Interview. Step one in the healing encounter is to talk with the person seeking healing in order to discover what the real need is. Does the person need healing, deliverance, or just counseling? Once the person's need is determined, a decision must be made on how to proceed with ministry, that is, what scriptural method should be used? At this point in the ministry engagement it is important that the Christian worker remain sensitive to the voice and leading of the Holy Spirit.

Step 2: Ministry Engagement. The Christian worker now acts based on his interview decision. He should ask the Holy Spirit to come and manifest His power. He can then minister healing through the laying on of hands, words of faith, commands of faith, declarations, petitions, teaching, the release of power, the prayer of agreement, binding and loosing, or some other biblical method. The Christian worker should remain constantly sensitive to what God is doing, watching for indications of the Spirit's work. He should at all times follow the Spirit's leading. Sometimes healing is a process and takes time (Mark 8:22-25). He should therefore continue to pray until the person is healed or he senses a release from the Spirit to stop.

Step 3: Post-prayer Guidance. Our ministry is not finished until we have given post-prayer guidance to the person we have just prayed for. Jesus often gave such guidance (Mark 5:19; John 5:14; 9:35-39). If the person has received healing, encourage him to continue in faith and obedience. If he is only partially healed, encourage him to trust God for the completion of the healing. If he doesn't receive healing, assure him of God's continuing love and Christ's healing power. Let him know that you will continue to pray and believe God with him for his healing.

How Jesus Healed the Sick

How did Jesus heal the sick? This is an important question because He is our example for ministry. As we observe the healing ministry of Jesus, we can discover a pattern for our own healing ministries. Jesus healed the sick in several ways:

1. By commanding the sick person to do something (Mark 3:5; Luke 7:14; John.5:8).
2. By commanding demons to leave (Mark 1:25; 5:8; Mark 9:25).
3. By speaking directly to the illness or condition (Matt. 8:3; Mark 7:34: 8:41; Luke 18:42).
4. By acknowledging of the faith of the recipient (Matt. 8:22).
5. By simply stating that the healing had taken place (Luke 13:12; John 5:50).

6. By touching or laying hands on the sick person (Matt. 8:15; 20:34; Mark 7:33-35; Luke 4:40).
7. By responding to faith (Matt. 10:52; 15:28; Mark 2:5).
8. By showing compassion (Matt. 14:14; Mark 1:41-42; Luke 7:13-15).
9. Through a release of power *(dunamis)* (Luke 6:19; 8:46).

The Name of Jesus

A careful examination of the healings performed by the disciples in the book of Acts shows that they often imitated and duplicated the methods of Jesus. There was, however, one important addition: they did it in the name of Jesus (Mark 16:17-18; Acts 4:10). Today we, too, should seek to imitate the methods of Jesus with this one essential addition—we must do it in the powerful Name of Jesus!

We, as Christ's disciples, have been commissioned to preach the gospel in all the world. Jesus has given us a clear model of how we must do this. Our job is to move out in simple faith and obedience, imitating His methods and expecting Him to confirm His Word with signs following.

Class Discussion

Discuss the following in class:
1. Define and discuss the importance of the proper "healing environment" in ministering to the sick.
2. Discuss the three steps in healing the sick as discussed in this lesson. Why is each step important?
3. List and discuss the healing methods of Jesus. Why is it important that we know how Jesus healed the sick?
4. Why should the healing minister not stop too soon in a healing engagement?
5. What counsel should be given if the person receives healing? If the person is only partially healed? If the person is not immediately healed?

How to Cast Out Demons

Central Truth
Spirit-filled disciples can be used by God to set people free from demonic bondage.

Lesson Outline
- Understanding Our Enemies
- How to Cast Out Demons

Introduction
As discussed in Lesson 3, demons strongly resist the coming of Christ's kingdom. They must, therefore, be challenged and defeated whenever they are encountered. This lesson will discuss how to cast out demons who have invaded the lives of those we encounter in ministry.

UNDERSTANDING OUR ENEMIES

Who are the Demons?
1. The origin and existence of demons. Most biblical scholars believe that demons are the angels who sinned and fell with Satan in his rebellion against God (Matt. 25:41; Rev.12:9). Jesus often confronted them and cast them out. He told His followers that they would do the same (Mark 16:17; Luke 9:1-2).

2. Characteristics of demons. Demons are actual living beings (Luke 4:33-35; 8:28-31; Acts 16:16-17; James 2:19) with intelligence and power (Luke 8:29; Acts 16:16-17; 2 Thess. 2:9). Because they do not have bodies (Gen. 3:1; Rev.16:13), they seek to dwell in the bodies of people. Unlike God who is uncreated and all powerful, they are created beings with limited power. They are morally perverted, absolutely evil, and cruel (Mark 1:23; Eph. 6:12).

3. Demonic objectives. Just as Christians seek to fulfill the will of their Heavenly Father, demons seek to fulfill the will of the devil. A key objective of demons is to strike out against people—and thus at God who created them in His own image—by gaining access to their bodies, souls, and spirits. They seek to hold people in bondage to fear, sickness, and enslaving habits. They further strive to deface the image of God in humans and to blind them to the truth of the gospel (Acts 10:38; 2 Cor. 4:4; 2 Tim. 2:25; Heb. 2:14).

Demonic Possession

Demons seek to afflict and control their victims in a number of ways. The most severe form of demonic affliction is called "demonic possession." When a demon (or demons) possesses an individual, he enters into that individual and takes control of his or her life. This control can be either partial or entire. It can be either continual or occasional. Demon possession manifests itself in many ways, including personality changes, the clouding of consciousness (Mark 9:26), another personality speaking through the afflicted person (Luke 8:28-30), extraordinary physical strength (Luke 8:29), unexplained knowledge or occultic powers (Acts 16:16-17), severe physical disturbances (Mark.1:26), deaf-mutism and blindness (Matt. 12:22-30; 9:32-34), suicidal and self-destructive tendencies (Mark 9:22, 5:5), and reaction to and fear of Christ or His name (Mark 1:24).

Although a Christian can be tempted, deceived, attacked, and even oppressed by demons from the outside, a Christian cannot be possessed, that is, inhabited by and taken control of at will by a demon. In Scripture there is no recorded instance of a born-again believer ever being demon possessed or having a demon cast out of him. And nowhere in the Epistles does demonic possession appear as a danger to which Christians are exposed, or about which Christians are warned.

Satan, A Defeated Foe

When confronting demons the Christian worker should keep in focus two powerful truths: that the power of the devil in this age is severely restrained by the presence of the Holy Spirit (2 Thess. 2:7), and that the power of Satan and his demons was broken at Calvary (John 12:31; Col. 2:15). The Spirit-filled believer who has submitted himself or herself to Christ and His work on the cross need never fear demons. They should confidently expect to defeat them anytime they encounter them.

HOW TO CAST OUT DEMONS

The Deliverance Minister

The deliverance minister must understand that the casting out of demons is an actual battle with real, malignant foes. He or she must never take the fight lightly. Because the battle is a spiritual one, the Christian worker must be filled with the Spirit and totally submitted to the will of God (James 4:7). He must know how to use his spiritual armor in battle. Further, the Christian worker must have a living faith in the victory of Calvary, the blood Christ, and the authority vested in Him.

Ministering Deliverance from Demons

Jesus is our example and guide in waging spiritual warfare (Luke 4:18-19; 31-37; Acts 10:38). He has commissioned and anointed us to minister deliverance to the captives (Mark 16:15-18). Through the empowering and gifts of the Holy Spirit we have been given power and authority to expose and expel demons (Luke 9:1-2; 10:17-19).

The Process of Deliverance

The casting out of demons is a sign of the presence and power of the kingdom of God and a demonstration of the lordship of Christ over His world. As in healing the sick, the following three elements are generally involved in deliverance:

1. The interview. If an interview is possible—and this is not always the case—then it is the first step in the deliverance process. During this discovery stage we may, through the gift of discerning of spirits, discover the demonic presence. Also, when agitated by the manifest presence of God, demons will sometimes expose themselves (Mark 1:23; 5:6-7).

It is good, when possible, to get a commitment from the one seeking deliverance before the actual deliverance begins. Lead him in a prayer of repentance and confession of sin, especially those sins closely related to his spiritual bondage. He should resolutely renounce the demonic infestation and the accompanying works of the flesh in his life.

2. Ministry engagement. We move into the actual power encounter with the demonic forces by calling on Jesus and asking for the Holy Spirit to come. Once we sense the presence of God, we can proceed to casting out (or in some cases, driving away) the demons.

One or more of the following procedures may be used: (1) The demons may be bound in the name of Jesus (Matt. 16:17-19; 18:18); (2) they may be commanded to come out, be gone, or loose their hold on their victim (Luke 4:35); and (3) they may be commanded not to reenter the person (Mark 9:25).

Sometimes the demons will resist and a struggle will result (Luke 8:29; 11:14). In such cases we should persist in faith until the victory comes. Deliverance is often accompanied by physical manifestations (Mark 7:30; Luke 4:33-35; 9:42). When this happens, we should not be intimidated nor distracted, but should continue to move in the power of the Spirit, order the demons to be quiet (Mark 1:25), and in the authority of Jesus' name, command them to come out and stay out (Mark 9:25).

3. Post-prayer guidance. When a person has been under the control of demons, follow-up counseling and prayer support is vital. The person will need much prayer and emotional support. If the person is not born again, he or she should immediately be lead to faith in Christ. Further, the person should be immediately led into the baptism in the Holy Spirit. Jesus warned about neglecting these essential matters (Matt. 12:43-45). The Christian worker should maintain close contact with the person until he or she is completely free from their bondage.

As followers of the Lord we have been commissioned to cast out demons. We must do this in the power and anointing of the Spirit, and in a way that shows loving concern for the dignity of the people we are ministering to. Our chief concern, however, should not be chasing demons but the proclamation of the life changing gospel of Christ!

Class Discussion

Discuss the following in class:
1. What is Satan's primary objective? How does he seek to carry out this objective?
2. Review and discuss five requisites for a deliverance minister.
3. If the person delivered is not saved or baptized in the Holy Spirit, what should be immediately done? Why is this important?
4. Review and discuss the three steps involved in casting out demons.

– Lesson 13 –
How to Pray with Believers to Be Filled with the Spirit

Central Truth
Every Spirit-filled believer can and should lead other believers into the baptism in the Holy Spirit.

Lesson Outline
- First Considerations
- How to Pray with Believers to Be Filled with the Holy Spirit

Introduction
In Lesson 6 we discussed how a person may personally receive the gift of the Holy Spirit. In this lesson we will take our discussion a step further; we will talk about how to lead others into this vital Christian experience.

FIRST CONSIDERATIONS

The person desiring to be used by God to lead others into the baptism in the Holy Spirit should understand the following scriptural truths about being filled with the Spirit:

Who Can Be Filled
Anyone who has been born again can and should immediately be filled with the Holy Spirit. This life-changing experience is not just for special or select Christians. The promise is for all believers of all ages (Acts 2:17-18; 38-39).

Who Can Pray with Others to Be Filled
Anyone who has himself or herself been filled with the Spirit can lead someone else into the experience. The chief requirement in praying for others to be filled with the Spirit is a sincere desire to see others blessed and used by God.

The Elements Involved

It is helpful understand five important spiritual elements involved in a person's being filled with the Holy Spirit:

1. Desire. Jesus said, "Blessed are those who hunger and thirst for righteousness, for they will be filled" (Matt. 5:6; see also Luke 11:9).

2. Faith. Faith is the prime ingredient in receiving anything from God, including the Holy Spirit. Jesus said that the Spirit would flow through "whoever believes" (John 7:38). Paul reminded the Galatian Christians that they had received the Holy Spirit "by believing what [they had] heard" (Gal. 3:2).

3. Prayer. The Holy Spirit is given in answer to believing prayer. Jesus said, "Ask, and it will be given to you" (Luke 11:9). He further taught, "Whatever you ask for in prayer, believe that you have received it, and it will be yours" (Mark 11:24).

4. Obedience. Peter said that God gives the Holy Spirit "to those who obey him" (Acts 5:32). He was talking specifically about those who will obey God and preach the gospel (vv. 29-32). God delights in empowering those who are ready to obey His command to share the gospel with the lost (Acts 1:8).

5. Yieldedness to God. Just as one being baptized in water yields himself or herself to the pastor, the one being baptized in the Holy Spirit must yield completely to Jesus. This yieldedness should include spirit, mind, body (Rom. 6:13; 12:1).

HOW TO PRAY WITH BELIEVERS TO BE FILLED WITH THE HOLY SPIRIT

As we did in the lessons on healing the sick and casting out demons, we suggest a three-step model in praying with believers to be filled with the Holy Spirit:

Step 1: The Interview

We begin the process of leading others into the baptism in the Holy Spirit by talking with them and explaining to them the meaning and purpose of the experience. Its purpose is to strengthen one's relationship with God and to empower believers to be effective witnesses for Christ (Acts 1:8). Answer any questions he may have. At this point we have two primary goals: to stir up expectant faith in the heart of the candidate and to bring him into an accurate understanding of what he must do and what he can expect to happen when he is prayed for. Assure the seeker that, if he is truly born again, God is ready now to fill him with the Holy Spirit.

Prayer Engagement

In the prayer engagement we lead the seeker into the actual experience of Spirit baptism. You may use the following procedure:

1. Lead the seeker in prayer. The prayer may proceed as follows, with the candidate repeating each line:

> Lord, I want to be your witness... I have, therefore, come to be empowered by your Spirit... You promised that everyone who asks, receives... I am asking, therefore, I expect to receive... When I begin to speak, I will release my faith... I will not be afraid... I will begin to pray in tongues as the Spirit gives me utterance.

After you have prayed, assure the candidate that God has heard his or her prayer, and that He is ready now to fill them with His Spirit. Encourage the candidate to be sensitive to the presence of the Spirit as He comes upon him. You may want to take a few moments to worship the Lord together and respond to His presence.

2. Lead the seeker in his or her step of faith. You may now ask the seeker to pray this simple prayer of faith with you: "Lord, right now, in Jesus' Name, I receive the Holy Spirit." This prayer provides a definite point where the seeker can focus his faith to receive the Holy Spirit. He should, at that moment, "believe that he has received." The moment the seeker believes, the Spirit will come and fill him. Encourage him to be aware the Spirit's coming. He may sense Spirit's presence deep inside.

The seeker should now act in bold faith and begin to speak—not from his mind, but from deep within, from where he senses God's Spirit inside (John 7:37-38). As he yields to the Spirit flowing into and through his being, he will begin to speak words he does not understand. This speaking will not be a forced effort, but a natural flow of supernatural words. Encourage the candidate not to be fearful but to cooperate fully with the Spirit by boldly speaking out in faith. If the candidate does not soon begin to speak in tongues, encourage him to continue yielding to the Lord. If he seems to have difficulty responding to the Lord, it is sometimes helpful to repeat the above procedure. As you do, point out how the seeker may more perfectly respond to the Spirit. Once he begins to speak in tongues, encourage him to continue on. Remain with him as long as he continues to pray in the Spirit.

Post-prayer Guidance

It is important that post-prayer counseling be given. If the candidate is filled with the Spirit, you will give one kind of counsel, if not, you will give another kind.

1. If the candidate is filled. Tell the candidate that receiving the Spirit is not an end in itself; it is rather a means to a greater end. You may say, "This is just the beginning. God will now begin to use you in powerful new ways. Go out right now and tell someone about Jesus!" You will want to add, "You should also spend time each day praying in the Spirit. This practice will give you strength and will remind you of the Spirit's presence within."

2. If the candidate is not filled. Assure him that the promise of Jesus is still true: "Everyone who asks receives" (Luke 11:10). Tell him that he should keep asking, and he will receive; he should keep seeking, and he will find, and he should keep knocking, and the door will be opened unto him (literal meaning of Luke 11:9). You may want to ask if he would like to pray again. If he does, repeat the above procedure, encouraging him to act in boldness and faith.

Class Discussion

Discuss the following in class:
1. Discuss five elements involved in a person's being filled with the Holy Spirit.
2. What ways may one use to inspire the seeker's faith to receive the Spirit?
3. What things could the Christian worker tell the seeker to increase his or her understanding about receiving the Spirit?
4. What post-prayer guidance should the candidate be given if he is filled with the Spirit? If he is not filled?

Spiritual Gifts Defined
1 Corinthians 12:1-10

Revelation Gifts: *Spirit-conferred insight; Given to know the mind of God*

- Word of knowledge: A Spirit-conferred revelation of a portion God's knowledge.
- Word of wisdom: A Spirit-conferred revelation of a portion God's wisdom.
- Discerning of spirits: A Spirit-conferred revelation of what S(s)spirit is being manifested or motivating an action.

Prophetic Gifts: *Spirit-inspired speech; Given to say the words of God*

- Gift of prophecy: A Spirit-inspired speaking forth of a message from God.
- Gift of tongues: A Spirit-inspired speaking forth of a message or prayer from God in a language not know by the speaker.
- Interpretation of A Spirit-inspired speaking forth of the meaning (interpretation) of a message or prayer given in tongues.

Power Gifts: *Spirit-energized works; Given to do the works of God*

- Gifts of healings: A Spirit-energized healing of diseases and infirmities.
- Gift of faith: A Spirit-energized surge of faith to accomplish a God-given task.
- Miraculous powers: (Gk: *energemata dunameon*) A Spirit-energized release of power to accomplish a God-ordained task.

– Other Books by Denzil R. Miller –

Power Ministry: How to Minister in the Spirit's Power (2004)
(also available in French, Portuguese, Malagasy, Kirnirwanda,
and Chichewa. Soon to be available in Urdu.)

*Empowered for Global Mission: A Missionary Look at
the Book of Acts* (2005)

From Azusa to Africa to the Nations (2005)
(also available in French, Spanish, and Portuguese)

Acts: The Spirit of God in Mission (2007)

In Step with the Spirit: Studies in the Spirit-filled Walk (2008)

*The Kingdom and the Power: The Kingdom of God:
A Pentecostal Interpretation* (2009)

*Experiencing the Spirit: A Study of the Work of the Spirit
in the Life of the Believer* (2009)

Teaching in the Spirit (2009)

*Power Encounter: Ministering in the Power and
Anointing of the Holy Spirit: Revised* (2009)
(Available in Kiswahili. Soon to be available in Spanish)

The 1:8 Promise of Jesus: The Key to World Harvest (2012)

All of the above books are available from the
Pneumalife Publications
3766 N. Delaware Avenue
Springfield, MO, 65803, USA
E-mail: denny.miller@agmd.org